Read for a Better World

EDUCATOR GUIDE Grades 2-3

By Tonya Leslie, PhD

Lerner Publications ◆ Minneapolis

Lerner Publications Company
An imprint of Lerner Publishing Group, Inc.
241 First Avenue North
Minneapolis, MN 55401 USA

For reading levels and more information, look up this title at www.lernerbooks.com.

Main body text set in Avenir LT Std.
Typeface provided by Adobe.

Manufactured in the United States of America
1-50155-49819-6/16/2021

Table of Contents

Introduction:
Reading for a Diverse World

We live in a diverse world. We see diversity in the variety of landscapes and ecosystems that exist on our planet. We hear diversity in the range of languages that are spoken around the world. We taste diversity in the mixes of spices that flavor the food we eat during cultural celebrations we share with family and friends. Often, books help us access this diverse world, taking us to places both real and imagined. Books bridge the gap so that we can visit and understand the lives of others, and through that exploration, we get closer to ourselves.

Children learn about the world through their experiences. Through interactions with adults, children understand their place in the world. Research shows that children first learn how to read the world at an early age, through the faces of their caregivers. Children look for connections through eye contact and facial expressions. Then, as children get older, they look for connections through other mediums, including texts.

As children get older, they look to texts to help them understand the larger world around them. They begin to wonder about their origins and their histories as they begin to see themselves within the frame of a larger world. As their curiosity expands, so does their appetite for knowledge. This is why it is important to expose children to a vast array of texts. They need access to both books that reflect their world and books that show them the larger world they exist within. They need to meet characters and worlds that are familiar and unknown as part of their own inquiry process around their lives. Every child needs opportunities to read books that reflect the beauty and the richness of our diverse world.

Learning for Justice Standards

Consider using the social justice anchor standards from Learning for Justice as a framework for developing your diverse library. These standards have four themes: identity, diversity, justice, and action. For more information, see www.learningforjustice.org/frameworks/social-justice-standards.

 IDENTITY

Books support the development of positive social identities through exploration and knowledge of self. With each new experience, children have the opportunity to refine their sense of self and recognize that their identity is always changing and developing.

 **DIVERSITY**

Books expose children to diverse stories, places, and perspectives that promote the development of empathy and respect for people who are both similar to and different from them.

 **JUSTICE**

Books expose children to stories about people who have fought for justice. We live in a complex world with a difficult history. When children learn that people have always resisted and fought against injustice, they recognize their own ability to treat others with dignity and respect.

 **ACTION**

Books encourage children to take actions in small ways that make a difference. For example, thinking about how to be a better friend or talking to loved ones in order to record family histories are ways children can practice leveraging their own responsibility for making the world a better place.

Diversifying Your Library

Research shows that a literacy-rich environment is important and that children who are exposed to books become more motivated and capable readers. In school and at home, access to books is critical, as children who are surrounded by books are more likely to become readers. School-based libraries are especially important for children who have limited access to books in their homes or communities.

Children need access to stories that represent aspects of their lived experience as well as stories that reflect the diversity of the world around them. Though representation in children's books has increased over previous years, there is still a surprising lack of diverse representation in children's texts relative to the diverse student population.

It is essential to consider what books are already in your library so you can offer not just more stories that feature diverse characters, but also feature a variety of stories and text types to ensure children are getting access to different stories and different ways of telling stories. Research suggests that books about diverse groups often have limited content. In these books, the same narrative is told again and again. So, what might seem like a diverse collection is just multiple iterations of the same story. For example, if the books in your collection tell only stories of Black leaders from the Civil Rights era, then you don't have a diverse collection. You just have a lot of books about one moment in history. The idea that only one story can be told about a group's experience reinforces stereotypes.

The idea that only one story can be told about a group's experience reinforces stereotypes.

Auditing Your Current Library

One way to consider the diversity of your library is by doing an audit. First, consider the students your library serves by asking yourself the following questions:

- What are the demographics of my students?

- What are the languages they speak at school and at home?

- What are some of the topics they are interested in?

Then, as you review the books in your collection, ask:

- Who is represented in this story?

- Who is this story about?

- What is this story about?

Consider how race, ethnicity, and gender show up in the books in your library. How many books feature Black characters? How many stories feature a girl as the main character? Once you quantify who shows up in the books you already have, now ask: What shows up? What is the story being told?

Audit your library with a count of the race, ethnicity, and gender of the main characters. If these aren't stated explicitly, look for clues in the pictures or character descriptions. Then, capture the story being told. Use this chart to help you audit your collection.

Title & Author	Ethnicity of Main Character	Race of Main Character	Gender of Main Character	Story Being Told

What surprised you about this audit?

_____

_____

_____

_____

Now consider the students in your class.
How does this library reflect them?

_____

_____

_____

_____

Do you notice patterns in the stories being told?
If so, what stories are overrepresented?

_____

_____

_____

_____

Consider This

This audit is a sample of types of representations to look for in your library. But it is important to also consider how other groups are represented within it. For example, while representations of disability have improved in the past decade, those representations are often stereotypical or negative. Consider how disability shows up in your collection. Are there any characters that have physical disabilities? What about learning disabilities or sensory disabilities? If there are characters with disabilities in your collection, are they the main character? Are they pitied or otherwise portrayed as incomplete or inadequate due to their disability?

Additional Resources to Help You Diversify Your Library

Sometimes it is challenging to know where to turn to find diverse books. There are many resources to help you find diverse books for your collection. Try these!

- **Lerner: Voices Matter—Celebrate Diverse Books**
lernerbooks.com/diversebooks

- **We Need Diverse Books**
diversebooks.org/

- **American Indians in Children's Literature**
americanindiansinchildrensliterature.blogspot.com/

- **Disability in Kidlit**
disabilityinkidlit.com/

Integrating Diversity into the Curriculum

You've done your audit. Now what? It's not enough to have diverse books on the shelf. You also need powerful instruction to engage readers! How do you engage children with these texts? How do you integrate these books into the curriculum? Diverse texts aren't meant to be "sometimes" books that are discussed only during certain holidays or celebrations. In fact, saving books to share during certain times of the year silences diverse voices throughout the year.

It is important to consider how you will weave these books into your daily instruction. As you consider big themes that you share with children (including the themes of identity, diversity, justice, and action), consider how to inspire children's curiosity so they will be interested in the books in this collection.

Teaching with diverse texts doesn't require you to know everything about a person, a culture, or even a country—but it does mean you have to go beyond your own comfort in order to offer a broad range of issues and topics.

Consider This

As you look for books to add to your library, consider ways to stay current on the latest books. Reading published reviews is one way to learn about new books. Following social media accounts of avid reviewers is another way to stay current. Ask yourself: What pathways have I created to discover more diverse books?

Notes

Other ways to include diverse books:

- Ask students to write six-word reviews of the books they read so that other students can get a quick introduction to the collection.

- Pair the texts in this collection with other texts children may engage with as part of the school's curriculum.

- Promote diverse stories through read aloud or quick book talks.

- Use curiosity as a tool to engage with texts.

Read for a Better World

Read for a Better World is a new kind of inclusive literacy collection designed for today's readers in today's world. Curated take-home and classroom bundles along with teacher resources and student activity books help students grow as readers and as people.

Dictionary for a Better World + Discussion Guide

A special edition of *Dictionary for a Better World: Poems, Quotes, and Anecdotes from A to Z* with a discussion guide provides an anchor across the collection.

Year-Round Take-Home Book Packs

Take-home packs culminating in summer reading help families build diverse, highly curated at-home libraries.

Student Action and Reflection Guides

Accelerate literacy with extension activities that deepen engagement around diversity, empathy, and historical and current events. The activities build cross-curricular skills.

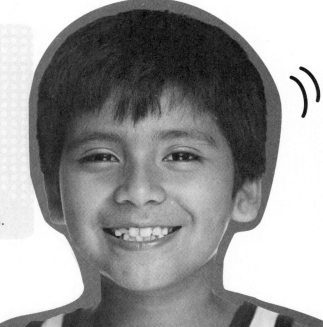

Where to Start

1. Set up your classroom library using the bins provided. You can download customizable bin labels at **LernerBooks.com/ReadBetter**.

2. Take a few minutes to familiarize yourself with the texts that are included in the classroom library. Each title was carefully selected by literacy and diversity experts to support the domains of identity, diversity, justice, and action, as defined by Learning for Justice. You can download a list of alignments and guided reading levels for each library at LernerBooks.com/ReadBetter.

3. Place your library wherever your students look for books for independent reading time. Decide whether you want to integrate Read for a Better World into your existing classroom library or keep it nearby as a dedicated library of its own.

4. Sign up for a free on-demand webinar introduction to Read for a Better World or register for personalized professional development sessions to help you implement Read for a Better World at **LernerBooks.com/ReadBetter**.

5. Begin with the first 30 pages of the Educator Guide, which will help you talk with your students about race, gender, ethnicity, and ability. This will help you use the different text types from the Read for a Better World Classroom Libraries to teach diversity, justice, identity, and action.

6. Conduct the classroom library audit on pp. 8–9 in the Educator Guide.

7. Review the Student Action and Reflection Guides as well as the lesson plans from the Educator Guide, and decide how to incorporate these lessons into your existing curriculum, during small group and independent reading time, or at special times throughout the day.

Looking to purchase student guides for a new school year?

Visit LernerBooks.com/ReadBetter to find them!

What Do We Mean by Diversity?

We've talked about diversity a lot, but we haven't really named what it is. *Diversity* is the type of word that is so broad it's hard to capture it in a definition. For the purpose of this book, we borrow from the definition of diversity as positioned by the advocacy organization We Need Diverse Books:

> **We recognize all diverse experiences, including (but not limited to) LGBTQIA, Native, people of color, gender diversity, people with disabilities*, and ethnic, cultural, and religious minorities.**
>
> *We subscribe to a broad definition of disability, which includes but is not limited to physical, sensory, cognitive, intellectual, or developmental disabilities, chronic conditions, and mental illnesses (this may also include addiction). Furthermore, we subscribe to a social model of disability, which presents disability as created by barriers in the social environment, due to lack of equal access, stereotyping, and other forms of marginalization.

This expansive definition is in response to calls for diversity in children's books that dates back to at least 1965, when literacy champion Nancy Larrick noted in a *Saturday Review* article titled "The All-White World of Children's Books" that many children of color—specifically Black children—were learning from books that omitted them entirely. She noted that most children's books featured only white characters, and when children of other races and ethnicities did show up in children's books, they were painted in stereotypical ways.

In the decades that followed, publishers and authors made strides to produce books that showed diverse children, but the gains were small. By 2019, the demand for diverse books led to the development of organizations like We Need Diverse Books that meant to push the industry forward. Some organizations began releasing statistics about the number of diverse books written by diverse creators. And while there has been some growth in the field, the numbers are still quite low.

Children's Books by Black, Indigenous, and Other Authors of Color Received by the Cooperative Children's Book Center (2018–2020)

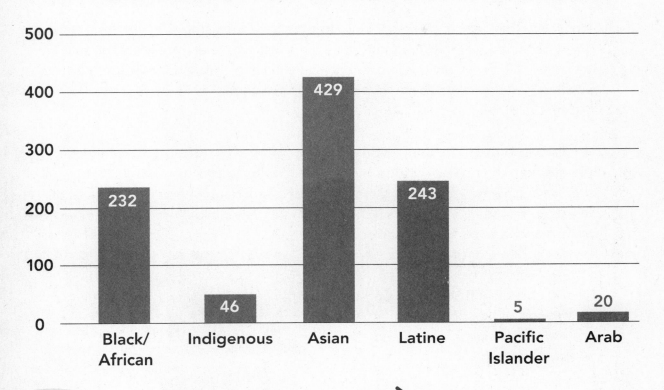

	Black/African	Indigenous	Asian	Latine	Pacific Islander	Arab
Value	232	46	429	243	5	20

"Students don't just need diverse literature because it's diverse. They need literature that inspires and awakens their potential to be the narrators of their own existence and to imagine a more just world."

—LATRISE JOHNSON, "STUDENTS DON'T NEED DIVERSE LITERATURE JUST BECAUSE IT'S DIVERSE"

Consider This

What is your definition of diversity?

Through Windows and Mirrors

One way to think about diverse texts is to consider the analogy of "windows and mirrors" coined by literacy expert Rudine Sims Bishop. When books are mirrors, they reflect the self. Children find resonance with characters who look, live, and think like they do. When these mirrors are positive and affirming, they can help children build positive self-images.

As windows, books transport children as they discover characters and cultures different from their own. Through windows, children explore other worlds and other ways of being—expanding their ideas and broadening their perspectives of the vastness of the world in which they live. In this way, children broaden their own horizons and see more examples of what they can aspire to. Through these types of books, children can journey to places real and unknown. Research suggests that this sort of perspective-shifting work is critical to building empathy and self-knowledge.

Diverse books are also important because they help children develop criticality. As children encounter unfamiliar representations of people and histories, they may bump up against their own unexamined beliefs. That is why it is imperative to engage children in criticality. According to literacy expert Gholdy Muhammad, criticality is the ability to read, write, and think in active ways to understand power, equity, anti-racism, and oppression. This type of thinking is different from passive learning, where children read and take in knowledge. Criticality is the act of investigating both the self and others in ways that help children build their capacity to be change agents in the world. This type of humanizing work intentionally centers histories, knowledge, and student reality as essential parts of their educational journey and engages children as active participants and co-constructors of knowledge. In this way, children interrogate their own history and stories as they encounter the history and stories of another.

With this lens, students can not only learn about and respond to injustice in the world around them, but they can also begin to think about injustice locally—in their own schools and communities.

However, it is also important to consider how windows and mirrors might not reflect positive images of children. Some children see distorted images of themselves in texts, and these interactions might cause them to disengage. Bishop warns that children who encounter only mirrors have an egocentric view of the world. This in turn constrains creativity. When children do not see the world as larger than themselves, they become isolated and intolerant.

"When youth have criticality, they are able to see, name, and interrogate the world not only to make sense of injustice but also to work toward social transformation."

—GHOLDY MUHAMMAD, *CULTIVATING GENIUS: AN EQUITY FRAMEWORK FOR CULTURALLY AND HISTORICALLY RESPONSIVE LITERACY*

"When children cannot find themselves reflected in the books they read, or when the images they see are distorted, negative, or laughable, they learn a powerful lesson about how they are devalued in the society of which they are a part. Our classrooms need to be places where all the children from all the cultures that make up the salad bowl of American society can find their mirrors."

—RUDINE SIMS BISHOP, "MIRRORS, WINDOWS, AND SLIDING GLASS DOORS"

Consider This

What does it look like to model teaching and learning as a humanizing act? How can books support that model?

Talking about Diverse Topics with Children

Diverse topics mean diverse conversations. Managing these kinds of topics requires a willingness to have conversations that talk explicitly and honestly about difference.

Talking Tips

- Practice having these conversations with another adult first. Try to imagine what questions a child might ask, and get comfortable answering them.

- Be prepared to be confronted with and reflect on your own biases.

- Give direct and honest answers. You may feel the need to provide lots of context on an issue when all a child needs is a simple response acknowledging their observations.

- Be aware of a child's emotions. Make sure you are discussing the topic in a way that leaves children feeling whole and validated.

Talking about Identity

Race, ethnicity, gender, ability, socioeconomic status, and religion are all elements of identity that can shape how children encounter and engage with their environment. They may see difference between themselves and their classmates. Sometimes these differences can be a source of classroom conflict. However, it is important for children to remember that essentially, we are all the same and have the same needs for safety and care. *Yaffa and Fatima: Shalom, Salaam* is the story of two neighbors, one Jewish and one Muslim, who care for one another during tough times. Books like *Yaffa and Fatima* can be great teaching tools for discussing the importance of friendship and empathy, and these discussions can help build a safe and inclusive classroom environment for all students.

Consider This

Humanizing language is a crucial tool when framing discussions around identity. People hold many identities that shape who they are, and using terminology that dilutes someone to a singular characteristic can be stigmatizing and negatively affect self-worth. Person-first language ("a woman with diabetes" rather than "a diabetic woman," for example) is one way people use humanizing language. But some people prefer identity-first language (i.e., "deaf man" rather than "man with deafness"). When talking about identity, it's important to understand why a community may have a general preference and to respect those preferences. Of course, each individual in a community is different, and it is always best to ask them how they would like to be identified.

Talking about Diversity

Children may notice visible differences among classmates, and have likely had conversations about respecting those differences. But diversity goes beyond what students see. When we talk about diversity, it is important to remember children have diverse ways of expressing themselves and diverse ways of learning. There is no one-size-fits-all. *Niko Draws a Feeling* is a good example of this diversity of expression. Niko makes drawings to visually represent complex or abstract feelings. Niko's way of expressing himself is different and sometimes misunderstood by his friends, family, and teachers. Then he meets a friend who sees the world the way he does. This story is a great reminder that we are all diverse in a variety of ways.

NIKO Draws a Feeling

Bob Raczka

illustrations by Simone Shin

Talking about Justice

By second and third grade, children have a strong understanding of fairness, and have even explored the difference between equality and equity—having equal resources versus having equal outcomes. Students at this age are beginning to have conversations about what equity looks like not just for individuals, but for groups of people who have faced discrimination, and how people have worked toward equity in numerous ways.

The Book Itch is about justice and the power of a dream. It tells a story of Lewis Michaux, who attempts to open a bookstore in Harlem specifically for Black people but is denied a loan because the banks had the mistaken belief that Black people didn't read. Michaux saves every penny he can and opens the bookstore anyway. The store grows into a community hub where people gather to read, talk, and share ideas for achieving liberation. It is a great example for students to see that sometimes justice—making things fair, and allowing people to have equal opportunity for resources—happens in everyday acts.

Consider This

Research suggests that children can experience racial bias early in childhood. For example, the Yale Child Study Center found that as early as preschool, teachers were more likely to observe and discipline Black boys than other children. This surveillance was due to teacher bias—not child behaviors. These patterns of bias can lead to the internalization of bias-based beliefs for all children—both about themselves and others. Therefore, it is important to talk to young children about race and fairness.

Talking about Action

At this age, children are beginning to look beyond their immediate environment and understand their place within a larger community. As they broaden their worldview, they may begin to notice problems within the community they are in and want to make a change. It's important to encourage students to develop their voice, and to convey that it is both acceptable and right that they participate in finding solutions that make their community a better place for everyone. The book *One Plastic Bag* helps to demonstrate these points. When Isatou Ceesay saw a problem in her community, she enlisted the help of the other women in her village and took action, recycling the plastic bags that littered their community into beautiful, crocheted bags. This book demonstrates how collective action can better the environment for everyone and is a good teaching tool for problem solving.

Diverse Text Types

We discussed the ways that diversity might show up in a text—through representations related to culture, race, and/or gender. But diversity is much broader than just the content of a collection. A good collection also has diverse text types that appeal to a wide variety of readers. The ways in which educators match children to texts matter. When children connect to a text, they grow as confident readers and writers. They also gain critical thinking skills. They can then use these skills to think about how to make the world more equitable for all.

Research suggests that students often prefer reading nonfiction over fiction. Still, most classroom libraries tend to feature fiction books, and school libraries generally tend to carry few informational texts. Text type is important. Informational texts provide context that informs lived experiences. Early exposure to informational texts gives children practice for the informational texts they will encounter in later grades. Informational texts build background knowledge and authentic, purposeful reading.

Research also suggests that culturally diverse children may find reading nonfiction texts more compelling. Perhaps that's because of the inherent diversity within nonfiction texts. Because they are informational, they provide new content and new ways of thinking about the known world. Nonfiction texts allow for rethinking and expanding knowledge. They also provide opportunities for different ways of engagement. It is easy to jump around a nonfiction text, skimming for content and interest, much in the way we read electronic texts on digital platforms.

"If we value all readers, we must value all reading."

—DONALYN MILLER, *READING IN THE WILD: THE BOOK WHISPERER'S KEYS TO CULTIVATING LIFELONG READING HABITS*

The Five Kinds of Nonfiction

One unique way to think about the types of texts children engage with is to consider classifying nonfiction texts into five distinct categories. This system of classification was devised by educator Melissa Stewart. She suggests that classification is important because it helps students to predict the type of information that will be presented in a book as well as identify the types of nonfiction books they most enjoy. The classification is also helpful for adults who are looking to match children to text. By understanding the types of nonfiction texts students are drawn to, educators can better choose other books to suggest for further reading.

The Read for a Better World collection includes the five kinds of nonfiction we know students love:

TRADITIONAL NONFICTION: These are great books to introduce children to a new subject. Presented with clear, straightforward language, these books are often part of a series and are great for use early on in a research process.

ACTIVE NONFICTION: Interactive and engaging, active nonfiction books are for the makers in the classroom. These activity-type books teach skills that can keep young readers engaged for hours.

BROWSEABLE NONFICTION: These visually appealing books are chock-full of great information that children can read cover to cover or skip around in. They are great for shared reading experiences.

NARRATIVE NONFICTION: Stories about real people or real events fall into this category. These books are often chronological in sequence and have real characters, real scenes, and engaging dialogue. They often appeal to fiction lovers.

EXPOSITORY LITERATURE: The creative presentation of a topic is a highlight of these types of nonfiction titles. These books provide more depth on a focused topic. Often, they are about specialized ideas like STEM concepts.

TRADITIONAL

Survey (all about) books

Overview of a topic

Often part of a large series

Clear, straightforward language

Expository writing style

Description text structure

EXPOSITORY LITERATURE

Focused topics presented creatively

Strong voice and rich, engaging language

Innovative format

Carefully chosen text structure

Expository writing style

Books about specialized ideas, such as STEM concepts

TRADITIONAL

EXPOSITORY LITERATURE

BROWSEABLE

NARRATIVE

ACTIVE

BROWSEABLE

Eye-catching design, lavishly illustrated

Short blocks of straightforward text

Can be read cover to cover or by skipping around

Great for shared reading

Expository writing style

Description text structure

ACTIVE

Highly interactive and/or teaches skills for engaging in activity

How-to guides, field guides, cookbooks, craft books

Clear, straightforward language

Expository writing style

NARRATIVE

Narrative writing style

Tells a story or conveys an experience

Real characters, scenes, dialogue, narrative arc

Strong voice and rich, engaging language

Chronological sequence structure

Books about people (biographies), events, or processes

The theory, tips, and audit in the previous pages should provide you with a strong foundation for building a diverse library and for talking about diverse subjects with your students. But it is just that—a foundation. You should continue to think about how you can build and maintain a literacy program where diversity is not simply a box to check off, but a critical element that is continuously developing and evolving alongside you.

Your audit will give you a baseline of what's in your library collection. While you may not need to do a full audit again, you should consider regularly pruning your library as part of an ongoing process to keep your collection updated and fresh. As you prune, plan to remove old, outdated, or redundant stories to make space for current books that are more diverse and are more representative of the children in your class. Use the findings from your audit to help you shop for particular types of stories.

The lesson plans that follow can be used with your Lerner collection or can be adapted to work with other books in your library. Each lesson includes space for you to take notes and reflect on how to best use the materials with your kids.

The research and discussion around diverse books have changed drastically in the past few decades, and they will continue to change in the future. Keep your ears and your heart open to new ideas that can improve and expand how your students read for a better world.

"We are different people with different needs, but underneath those differences, we are . . . humans striving for happiness. We are joined by our belief that all people deserve the same opportunity to follow their dreams and experience the world, no matter how different they are from one another."

—IRENE LATHAM AND CHARLES WATERS, *DICTIONARY FOR A BETTER WORLD*

Notes

Resources

- Aronson, K., Callahan, B., and O'Brien, A. (2017). Messages matter: Investigating the thematic content of picture books portraying underrepresented racial and cultural groups. *Sociological Forum*, *33*(1), 165-185. https://onlinelibrary.wiley.com/doi/abs/10.1111/socf.12404.

- Cress, S. W. & D. T. Holm (1998). Developing empathy through children's literature.

- Duke, N. K. (2000). 3.6 minutes per day: The scarcity of informational texts in first grade. *Reading Research Quarterly*, *35*(2), 202-224.

- Kuhn, K. E., C. M. Rausch, T. G. McCarty, S. E. Montgomery & A. C. Rule (2017). Utilizing nonfiction texts to enhance reading comprehension and vocabulary in primary grades. *Early Childhood Education Journal, 45*(2), 285-296.

- Mallan, K. (2013). Empathy: Narrative empathy and children's literature. In *(Re)imagining the World* (pp. 105-114). Springer.

- McKnight, D. M. (2010). Overcoming 'ecophobia,': fostering environmental empathy through narrative in children's science literature. *Frontiers in Ecology and the Environment, 8*(6), e10-e15.

- Muhammad, G. E. (2019). Protest, power, and possibilities: The need for agitation literacies. *Journal of Adolescent and Adult Literacy, 63*(3), 351-355.

- Muhammad, G. E. & N. Behizadeh (2015). Authentic for whom?: An interview study of desired writing practices for African American adolescent learners. *Middle Grades Review*, *1*(2), 1-18.

Endnotes

6. Neuman, S. and Moland, N. (2019). Book deserts: the consequences of income segregation on children's access to print. *Urban Education*, *54*(1), 126–147. https://journals.sagepub.com/doi/pdf/10.1177/0042085916654525.

14. "About Us," We Need Diverse Books, accessed March 10, 2021, https://diversebooks.org/about-wndb/.

14. Larrick, N. (1965). The all-white world of children's books. *The Saturday Review*, 63-65.

15. Data on books by and about Black, Indigenous and People of Color published for children and teens compiled by the Cooperative Children's Book Center, School of Education, University of Wisconsin-Madison. 16 Apr. 2021. https://ccbc.education.wisc.edu/literature-resources/ccbc-diversity-statistics/books-by-and-or-about-poc-2018/. Accessed 8 June 2021.

For more information on talking to students about diversity, visit lernerbooks.com/challenge?gid=335.

Access code: BetterWorld

15. Johnson, L. (2016, April 12). Students don't need diverse literature just because it's diverse. *Field Notes*. National Council of Teachers of English. https://ncte.org/blog/2016/04/students -dont-need-diverse-literature-just-diverse/.

16. Bishop, R. S. (1990). Mirrors, windows, and sliding glass doors. *Perspectives: Choosing and Using Books for the Classroom*, 6(3), ix-xi.

17. Muhammad, G. (2020). *Cultivating Genius: An Equity Framework for Culturally and Historically Responsive Literacy*. Scholastic.

21. Gilliam, W. S., A. N. Maupin, C. R. Reyes, M. Accavitti & F. Shic. (2016). Do early educators' implicit biases regarding sex and race relate to behavior expectations and recommendations of preschool expulsions and suspensions? Yale University Child Study Center.

23. Goodwin, B. and Miller, K. (2012). Research says nonfiction promotes student success. *Educational Leadership*, 70(4), pp. 80-82. https://www.ascd.org/publications/educational -leadership/dec12/vol70/num04/Nonfiction-Reading-Promotes-Student-Success.aspx.

23. Leal, D., and Moss, B. (1999). Encounters with information text: Perceptions and insights from four gifted readers. *Reading Horizons: A Journal of Literacy and Language Arts, 40*(2). https://core.ac.uk/download/pdf/144154483.pdf.

23. Miller, D., & Kelley, S. (2013). *Reading in the Wild: The Book Whisperer's Keys to Cultivating Lifelong Reading Habits*. Jossey-Bass.

23. Young, T. A., Moss, B., & Cornwell, L. (2007). The classroom library: A place for nonfiction, nonfiction in its place. *Reading Horizons: A Journal of Literacy and Language Arts, 48*(1). https://scholarworks.wmich.edu/reading_horizons/vol48/iss1/3.

24. Stewart, M., & Correia, M. P. (2021). *5 Kinds of Nonfiction: Enriching Reading and Writing Instruction with Children's Books*. Stenhouse Publishers.

27. Latham, I., & Waters, C. (2020). *Dictionary for a Better World: Poems, Quotes, and Anecdotes from A to Z*. Carolrhoda Books.

Notes

Notes

Identity

Understanding Identity

Students are more successful in the classroom and in life when they feel free to be their full selves. However, children are still in the process of constructing their identities. Give students the chance to experiment with identity and what it means by providing opportunities to explore sense of self. Encourage students to examine the many different aspects of their own and their peers' identities. Create a safe space where they can learn to challenge assumptions they may make about others. And most importantly, help students in your class foster a sense of pride and self-esteem surrounding their own identities.

Tips & Considerations

- Remember that identity is fluid, especially in children. Their behavior might change from day to day as they grow into their true selves.

- Be aware of any biases you may hold. At this age, your students may not consciously be part of any group. They may not identify with how they appear. Do not make assumptions about students' identities. Instead, allow them to self-identify.

- Allow your classroom makeup to guide your approach to identity discussions. Pay attention to the ways your students express their identities and what they are noticing about one another. Consider how their behaviors at home may differ from their behaviors in the classroom.

- It's natural for children to notice differences. However, avoid "othering" when talking about differences or framing certain cultural groups or characteristics as the default.

- It can be helpful to provide examples from your own life when discussing identity and unpacking assumptions. However, avoid always defaulting to your own experience or the experiences of students in majority groups.

Questions to Ask

What languages do my students speak?

_____

_____

What is the gender makeup of my students?

_____

_____

Where are my students and their families from?

_____

_____

What religions are represented by my students?

_____

_____

How am I engaging parents to learn more about the students in my class?

_____

_____

Invisible Identities

Explore the concept of inner and outer identities by helping your students explore their classmates' hopes and dreams.

What You Need

- ❑ Dry-erase board and markers
- ❑ *Who Is a Scientist?* by Laura Gehl
- ❑ Hopes and Dreams worksheet for each student (p. 37)
- ❑ Writing supplies for students

Learning Goals

- Understand the different aspects that make up a person's identity
- Identify examples of inner and outer characteristics
- Explore the idea that everyone has dreams, interests, and aspirations that can't be learned just by looking at a person

Words to Know

aspiration: a hope or goal

characteristic: a feature or quality of somebody or something

Key Questions

- What can I learn about someone else's identity based on how they look?
- How can I learn about the invisible parts of someone's identity?
- What can't I know about someone by looking at them?
- How do hopes, dreams, and aspirations contribute to someone's identity?

Talk about It

Begin by introducing the concepts of identity and of characteristic. Explain that some characteristics are invisible.

Say It

"Identity is the collection of all the little things that make you who you are. Your identity is made up of different characteristics. This is a bit like the ingredients in a recipe. Each ingredient is important on its own. But when you combine them together, you get something wonderful and unique.

"Your personality, what you believe, and the way you look are all characteristics. Some characteristics are things people can see, like being tall or having curly hair. Other characteristics are invisible. These are things people wouldn't know just by looking at you, like what you care about or what you hope for. For example, you might love animals and hope one day to be a veterinarian.

"Today we are going to learn more about the hopes, dreams, and aspirations that make us each unique!"

Try It

Have students explore different aspects of identity as a group and in pairs.

1. As a class, study the pictures on pages 10–11, 12–13, 20–21, and 26–27 of *Who Is a Scientist?* by Laura Gehl without reading it. Ask students to list characteristics about each person based on looking at the photos. Write students' answers on the board. Remind them that these characteristics can be physical traits or personality traits, such as likes or dislikes.

2. If needed, ask students questions to encourage them to look more closely at the photos. For example, *Munazza is wearing a hijab in both photos. What does this tell you about her?*

3. Now go back and read the descriptions of each person. Ask students to list the characteristics they learned about each person based on the descriptions. Circle any characteristics that are on your original list. Write down any new invisible characteristics.

4. Divide your class into random pairs. Give each student a copy of the Hopes and Dreams worksheet. Encourage students to ask their partner questions to learn about what interests them and what type of job they hope to have when they grow up. Then have students draw portraits of their partners expressing part of their identity.

Think about It

Come back together as a class. Invite students to share what they learned about their partners. Did anything surprise them?

SEL Connection

Understanding what sparks a child's interest is key to building connection. Demonstrate to students that you care about their goals and believe in their ability to achieve them. Using positive language throughout this discussion will help support students' belief in themselves and their abilities.

Notes

Hopes and Dreams

My name: _____

This is _____.

They are inspired by _____.

They are interested in _____ and _____.

When they grow up, they hope to _____

_____.

Inner Self Self-Portrait

Invite students to explore their inner selves by creating their own Frida Kahlo-style self-portrait.

What You Need

- ❑ Screen to show images of Frida Kahlo and her paintings
- ❑ Outer Me/Inner Me worksheet for each student (pp. 41–42)
- ❑ Drawing supplies, including markers, paints, or other colorful mediums

Learning Goals

- Introduce Frida Kahlo and her self-portraits
- Identify ways each student's inner self differs from their outer selves
- Help students express their inner selves through artwork

Key Questions

- What aspects of my inner self can people not see by looking at me?
- What thoughts, feelings, and emotions make up my inner self right now?
- What do I wish people knew about my inner self?

Consider This

Additional examples of Kahlo's self-portraits can be found at www.fridakahlo.org. Note that some of Kahlo's work features nudity or violent imagery students may find distressing. Be sure to screen images before showing them to your class.

Talk about It

Begin by reminding students that identities are made of characteristics people can see, such as having brown eyes or being able to run fast. Other parts of their identities are hidden, such as loving to sing in private.

Show students a photo of Frida Kahlo, and read a short biography of her.

Say It

"Frida Kahlo was a famous Mexican artist. When she was a teenager, Kahlo was in a bus accident, which severely injured her. Kahlo spent many months in bed as she recovered. During this time, she painted many stunning self-portraits. She once said, 'I paint self-portraits . . . because I am the person I know best.' Kahlo's self-portraits allowed others to experience her inner thoughts and feelings. Kahlo often painted in a fantastic and dreamlike style of art."

Show students an image of Kahlo's painting *Self-Portrait with Thorn Necklace and Hummingbird*. You can find the painting at www.fridakahlo.org/self-portrait-with -thorn-necklace-and-hummingbird.jsp.

Ask students to imagine what inner thoughts and feelings Kahlo might be trying to express with this self-portrait.

Then, read the following description of the painting paraphrased from the same website:

Say It

"Frida Kahlo used many symbolic creatures in this painting. These symbols represent her feelings. Birds often symbolize freedom and life. Hummingbirds are usually colorful and hover above flowers. But in this painting, the hummingbird is black and lifeless. This might be a symbol of Kahlo herself. Kahlo spent most of her life in physical pain after her bus accident. This painting uses symbols to express her pain."

Try It

Give each student a copy of the Outer Me/Inner Me worksheet. Explain that the Outer Me side should be used to draw a realistic self-portrait of themselves. (Alternatively, teachers could take photos of students to use for this portion.) On the Inner Me side, students should create a self-portrait that expresses their inner thoughts and feelings. Encourage them to use the same dreamlike and fantastic style as Kahlo. Remind them they can include symbols, like plants or animals, to represent certain aspects of their emotions.

Think about It

Discuss the activity as a class. Invite students to share how creating their self-portraits made them feel:

- *How did it feel to express your inner self through art?*
- *How did your inner self-portrait differ from your outer self-portrait?*
- *What symbols did you choose to help represent your inner self?*

Notes

Outer Me

What do people see when they look at you?

Name: _____

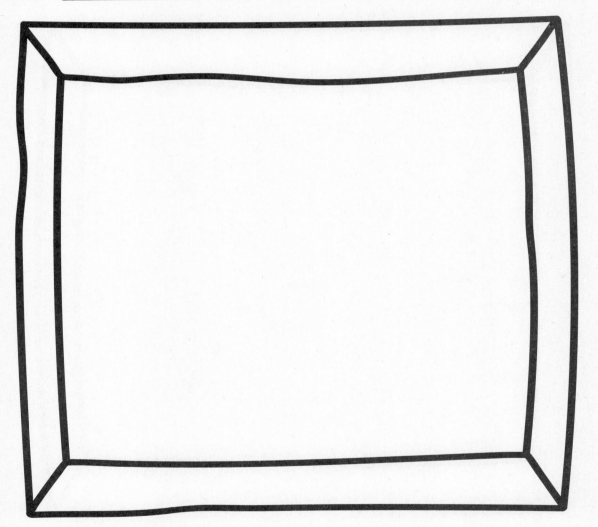

When people look at me, they see _____

_____

_____ .

Inner Me

What don't people see about you when they look at you?

Name: _____

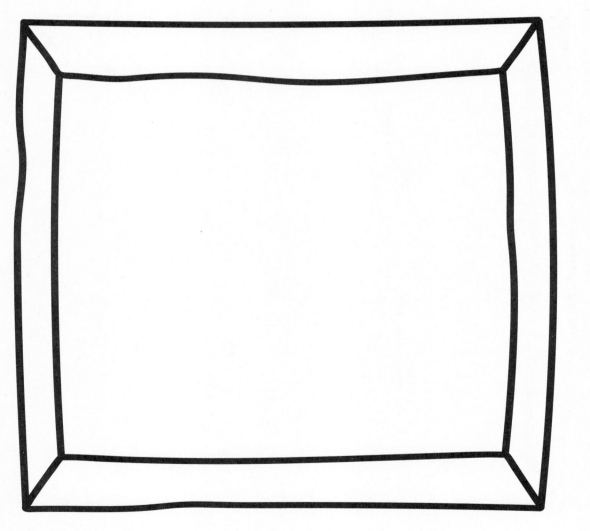

One thing people don't know about me is _____

_____. I am _____

_____ and _____.

Confident in Me!

Explore the concepts of self-esteem and positive body image by learning about ballet dancer Misty Copeland.

What You Need

❑ *Misty Copeland: Principal Ballerina* by Heather E. Schwartz

Learning Goals

- Understand the relationship between health and body image
- Learn about Misty Copeland's struggles with body image and self-esteem

Key Questions

- What does it mean to be healthy?
- What are some ways to be healthy?

Talk about It

Explain why health is important and how it relates to body image.

Say It

"People often think being healthy means eating well and exercising. But health is much more than that. Your health is your overall well-being. This includes your physical body, but it also includes how you feel emotionally, mentally, and socially. Health also includes the way you think about your body. This is called body image. There are lots of reasons to improve your health. Being healthy can put you in a good mood and give you more energy. Having a healthy body image can also improve your confidence in yourself!"

Next, introduce students to Misty Copeland.

Say It

"Misty Copeland is an American ballet dancer. In 2015, Copeland made history as the first Black woman to be a principal dancer with the American Ballet Theatre. Throughout her career, Copeland has overcome unfair treatment because of her skin color. She has also been treated unfairly because her body type is different from many other professional ballet dancers."

Try It

1. Read pages 14–15 of *Misty Copeland: Principal Ballerina by Heather E. Schwartz*, including the page 15 quote from Copeland.

2. Discuss what you read as a class. Ask the following questions to encourage discussion:

- *What do you think being healthy means to Misty Copeland?*
- *What health goal did Misty Copeland set for herself?*
- *How does Misty Copeland's acceptance of herself help her enjoy dance more?*

Think about It

Invite your class to share ways they stay healthy. Remind them that health includes body, mind, and emotions.

SEL Connection

For many children, body image is inextricably tied to self-esteem. Toddlers and very young children are delighted by their bodies and what they can do. By the time students reach elementary school, they begin comparing their own bodies with their peers. Helping students foster a positive body image will improve their confidence in themselves and their abilities. Encourage positive body image by showing images of bodies of all shapes and sizes when providing exemplars to your class.

Notes

Helpful Resources

Encouraging a Healthy Body Image
kidshealth.org/en/parents/body-image.html

Eyes that Kiss in the Corners by Joanna Ho

Flora and the Flamingo by Molly Idle

The Most Beautiful Thing

Help students explore what makes their families special.

What You Need

- ❏ *The Most Beautiful Thing* by Kao Kalia Yang
- ❏ The Most Beautiful Thing worksheet for each student (p. 49)
- ❏ Drawing supplies for students

Learning Goals

- Understand that families come in many different shapes and sizes
- Reflect on what makes students' families special

Key Questions

- What is a family?
- How is my family unique?
- What is my favorite part about my family?

Talk about It

Explain that today you will be talking about families and exploring ways your students' families are special.

Consider This

Family situations can be fluid. A student may have a parent who is living away from home whom they miss. A student with an absent or incarcerated parent may be embarrassed about their family situation. Highly mobile students may feel their family situation is unstable. Pay attention to students who seem withdrawn or act out during this lesson. Try to avoid framing certain types of family structures as "traditional" or "normal," which could make students feel othered. Rather than focusing on who is in a student's family, focus on the ways the people in their family love and support one another and how the students show their own love and support.

Say It

"Families are groups of people who love and care for each other. Families come in all shapes and sizes. Sometimes people in families live together, and sometimes they live apart. People who aren't related to you can still be part of your family."

Try It

1. Read aloud *The Most Beautiful Thing* by Kao Kalia Yang. Discuss the book as a class. Ask the following questions:
   - *Why does Kalia think her grandmother's smile is the most beautiful thing?*
   - *What do you think Kalia's grandmother's smile represents to Kalia?*
   - *How do Kalia's grandmother's stories help Kalia appreciate her family?*
   - *What other clues does the book give you about Kalia's family?*
2. Give each student a copy of The Most Beautiful Thing worksheet.
3. Give students time to fill out the worksheet and draw a family portrait highlighting what makes their families unique.
4. Divide students into groups of three or four. Invite students to share their portraits with their groupmates, discussing the most beautiful thing in each student's family.

Tip for Teachers

Provide an example by sharing the most beautiful thing in your family.

Think about It

Come back together as a group and reflect on the diversity of the families in your classroom. Hang the portraits in a gallery where students can view them.

SEL Connection

Much of a child's early worldview is shaped by the caregivers in their family. Children watch these adults make decisions, interact with others, and decide what is right and wrong. Each child's unique identity is in part influenced by the adults who care for them. Encouraging students to be proud of their identities can also help foster a deeper connection between students and the family members who care for them.

Notes

The Most Beautiful Thing

Name: _____

The most beautiful thing about my family is _____

_____,

because _____

_____.

Guess that Feeling!

Explore feelings and help your students discover healthy ways to express their emotions.

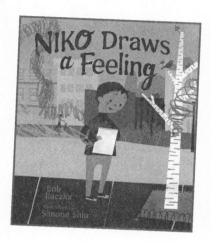

What You Need

- ❑ *Niko Draws a Feeling* by Bob Raczka
- ❑ Shoebox or similarly sized opaque container
- ❑ Slips of paper with feelings written on them, such as happy, excited, overwhelmed, etc.; one for each student
- ❑ Scrap paper and drawing supplies for each group of three or four students
- ❑ Timer
- ❑ Dry-erase board and markers

Learning Goals

- Visually express a feeling
- Identify healthy ways to express feelings

Key Questions

- What are feelings?
- What are some healthy ways to express feelings?
- How do I express my feelings?

Consider This

Children at this age are still learning to regulate emotions, and that's okay. Avoid labeling feelings as good or bad. Instead, focus on the ways students experience and express their feelings.

Tip for Teachers

Most psychologists consider feelings to be the conscious experience of emotional reactions. However, the terms *feeling* and *emotion* are often used interchangeably, especially when discussed with children.

Talk about It

Introduce the concept of feelings.

Say It

"Everyone has feelings. Sometimes feelings can be overwhelming. These feelings can lead you to do or say things you wouldn't normally. But all feelings are important! They give you information about how you feel about what is going on around you. It's important to share your feelings with others instead of keeping them inside. Paying attention to your feelings and expressing them can help you make sense of them."

Try It

1. Read aloud *Niko Draws a Feeling* by Bob Raczka.

2. Place the slips of paper in a box and have each student draw one at random. Instruct them not show anyone what's written on their slip of paper.

3. Divide students into groups of three or four. Give each group several sheets of scrap paper and drawing supplies.

4. Explain that you will be playing "Guess that Feeling." One student in each group will draw the feeling they picked, just like Niko. The student drawing isn't allowed to write words, letters, or symbols. They also cannot speak or gesture. The other group members will have three minutes to try and guess the feeling! Repeat the game until each group member has drawn their feeling.

Think about It

Come back together as a class and connect the activity back to the importance of expressing feelings.

Drawing is just one way to express how you are feeling. What are some other ways you can express feelings?

Write your students' responses on the dry-erase board.

Notes

Helpful Resources

The Boy with Big, Big Feelings by Britney Winn Lee

Emotions & Self-Awareness
www.pbs.org/parents/learn-grow/all-ages/emotions-self-awareness

How to Teach Kids About Their Feelings
www.verywellfamily.com/how-to-teach-kids-about-feelings-1095012

Finding Strengths

Teach children to recognize their own strengths as they learn about Cherokee engineer Mary Golda Ross.

What You Need

- ❑ *Classified: The Secret Career of Mary Golda Ross, Cherokee Aerospace Engineer* by Traci Sorell
- ❑ Dry-erase board and markers
- ❑ Finding My Strengths worksheet for each student (p. 55)

Learning Goals

- Identify the difference between character traits and skills
- Identify students' individual strengths

Key Questions

- What character traits help me overcome challenges?
- What skills am I proudest of?

Talk about It

Tell students that today you will be talking about strengths.

Say It

"Strengths can be both skills and character traits. Skills are things you do well. You also have character traits. These are the qualities that make you who you are. Character traits can include kindness, generosity, and honesty."

Explain that you are going to be learning about Mary Golda Ross. As you read, ask students to pay attention to the strengths that helped Ross achieve her goals and overcome challenges.

Try It

1. Read aloud *Classified: The Secret Career of Mary Golda Ross, Cherokee Aerospace Engineer* by Traci Sorell.

2. After reading, ask your class to brainstorm a list of Ross's strengths. Write their answers on the dry-erase board.

   Review your list with your class. Ask:
   - *Is this strength a skill or a character trait?*
   - *How did this strength help Ross?*

3. Give each student a copy of the Finding My Strengths worksheet. Give them a few minutes to fill the worksheets out on their own. Then divide the class up into pairs. Ask them to share their strengths and character traits with their partners. Do their partners have anything to add to these lists?

Think about It

Come back together as a class and discuss where strengths come from.

Some character traits are learned from our families or cultures, such as how Ross learned the values of teamwork and humility from her Cherokee upbringing. Where are some other places our strengths come from?

Notes

Finding My Strengths

Name: _____

My Character Traits	My Skills
⊙	☆
_____	_____
✳	✳
_____	_____
☆	⊙
_____	_____
●	●
_____	_____
✳	☆
_____	_____
☆	✳
_____	_____

Understanding Diversity

For students to be thoughtful, collaborative, and respectful citizens of their communities and the world, it is essential for them to cultivate a diverse worldview. A diverse worldview is one that acknowledges the many ways people look, dress, eat, work, grieve, worship, and more. It means accepting and respecting these differences, approaching them with curiosity, and harnessing their collective strength.

To encourage a diverse worldview, reflect on your own worldviews and cultural frames of reference. How do they differ from those of your students? How might you try to uncover your unconscious biases to help your students feel seen, heard, and safe?

Tips & Considerations

- Children notice differences but are often discouraged from doing so. While it's important to recognize our many commonalities, it's just as critical to frame differences as things to be acknowledged and celebrated.

- Learning takes place when students feel socially accepted and safe. Cultivating trust and rapport with students is essential to creating a safe learning environment. One way to foster trust is sharing vulnerable moments with students; tell them about times you faced challenges or made mistakes.

- Be aware of the cultural backgrounds that undergird your students' behaviors, as well as your own cultural background, which influences the way you respond to students' behaviors.

Questions to Ask

How are my students and I the same? How are we different?

_____

_____

One thing about my students that surprises me is:

_____

_____

What kinds of expectations do I have for my students? How do I respond when students don't meet these expectations?

_____

_____

One thing I think is really important in a classroom is:

_____

_____

How can I create a sense of trust and safety in my classroom?

_____

_____

Diversity

Different and the Same

Help students discover how they are similar to and different from one another.

What You Need
- ❏ Dry-erase board and markers
- ❏ Classmate Interview worksheet for each student (p. 60)

Learning Goals
- Acknowledge the many ways we differ from one another
- Understand that diversity makes the world more interesting and beautiful
- Understand that despite our differences, we have much in common

Key Questions
- How do my classmates and I differ from one another?
- What do my classmates and I have in common?
- Why is it important that we are not all the same?

Consider This

When talking about difference, be careful not to imply there is a default "normal" to be different from. This can come down to small phrasing choices, such as saying, "What are some ways we differ from one another?" instead of, "What are some ways others may differ from you?"

Talk about It

Establish that there are many ways in which we differ from one another. Ask students to think of some ways we differ. Write their thoughts on the dry-erase board.

Tell students they are going to partner up and do interviews to get to know each other better.

Try It

Have students interview each other to learn more about their similarities and differences.

1. Give each student a Classmate Interview worksheet.

2. Put students in pairs. Have students take turns interviewing their partners.

3. Once every pair has completed both their interviews, place students into new pairings. Repeat the interview process in this second group.

4. Gather for group reflection.

Think about It

Ask students to share some things they and their partners had in common.

Ask students to share some ways they and their partners differed from one another.

Ask students why they think it's a good thing that we're not all the same.

Notes

Classmate Interview

Ask your first partner the questions below. Write their answers in the spaces provided.

My name: _____

~~~~~~

What is your name? _____

What is your favorite meal? _____

What is your favorite season? _____

What is your favorite thing to learn about? _____

_____

What is your favorite game? _____

~~~~~~

Ask your second partner the questions below. Write their answers in the spaces provided.

What is your name? _____

What is your favorite meal? _____

What is your favorite season? _____

What is your favorite thing to learn about? _____

_____

What is your favorite game? _____

Belonging to a Diverse Nation

Use an American's immigration story to discuss belonging to a diverse nation.

What You Need

- ❑ *Pavel and the Tree Army* by Heidi Smith Hyde
- ❑ My Country and Me worksheet for each student (p. 63)
- ❑ Writing and drawing supplies for students

Learning Goals

- Understand what it means to belong to a country
- Understand that differences make a country great

Key Questions

- What does it mean to belong to a country?
- How can I use my own skills and strengths to make my country better?

Talk about It

Tell students you are going to read the book *Pavel and the Tree Army* by Heidi Smith Hyde. Ask them to think about what Pavel and his friends learn about being American.

Think about It

Ask students to share their thoughts. *What did Pavel learn in the book?*

Prompt students to reflect on what it means to belong to a country. *What do you think makes Pavel a real American?*

Say It

"Pavel learned that being a real American isn't about being born in the country. It isn't about speaking a certain way or knowing the words to the national anthem. Pavel learned he was a real American because he wanted to live in America, and he worked to make the country a better and more beautiful place."

Try It

Invite students to reflect on what they might contribute to their country.

1. Give each student a copy of the My Country and Me worksheet.

2. Read aloud the worksheet's introduction: *Every country is made up of individuals with different skills and strengths. Our differences make our nations better than they would be without us!*

3. Ask students to reflect on how they, like Pavel, can use their skills and strengths to make their country a better place. Have them share their thoughts on the worksheet.

4. Once everyone has finished the activity, invite students to share their answers with the group.

Notes

SEL Connection

Discussing what it means to belong to a group helps develop students' social awareness, enhancing their ability to understand and accept others' perspectives as well as recognize others' strengths. When students reflect on their own skills and strengths, they develop a sense of self-efficacy and engage with their unique roles and contributions to their communities.

✳ My Country and Me

Every country is made up of individuals with different skills and strengths. Our differences make our nations better than they would be without us!

Name: _____

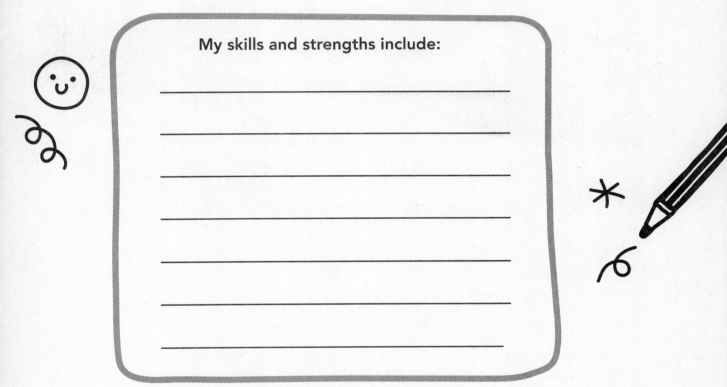

My skills and strengths include:

_____

_____

_____

_____

_____

_____

I can use my skills and strengths to make my country better by

_____

_____

_____.

Remembering the Past

Teach students about remembering the past using Juneteenth as an example.

What You Need

- ❑ *Juneteenth* by Vaunda Micheaux Nelson and Drew Nelson
- ❑ Dry-erase board and markers

Learning Goals

- Learn about the Juneteenth holiday
- Understand the importance of remembering the past

Key Questions

- What is Juneteenth and what does it celebrate?
- Why is it important to remember the past?

Talk about It

Tell students you are going to read a book about the holiday Juneteenth. Ask students to share what they know about Juneteenth.

Read aloud the book *Juneteenth* by Vaunda Micheaux Nelson and Drew Nelson.

Talk about key terms and concepts surrounding Juneteenth using Who, What, When, Where, Why, and How. Write students' thoughts on the dry-erase board. Your lists should look similar to the following:

WHO was involved?

- Enslaved Black Americans
- President Abraham Lincoln
- General Gordon Granger

WHAT happened?

- Enslaved people learned they were free

WHEN did the holiday originate?

- June 19th, 1865

WHERE did the holiday originate?

- Galveston, Texas

WHY is Juneteenth a holiday?

- To remember the past
- To celebrate freedom

HOW do people celebrate Juneteenth?

- Barbecues
- Picnics
- Red velvet cake
- Red drinks

- Parades
- Baseball games
- Dancing
- Prayer services

- Reading the Emancipation Proclamation
- Telling stories of enslavement and freedom

Think about It

Reflect on the importance of remembering the past.

Juneteenth takes place today because of what happened in America's past. Why do you think it is important to remember what happened in the past?

Notes

Helpful Resources

Teaching Juneteenth
www.learningforjustice.org/magazine/teaching-juneteenth

The Coming of Freedom: Celebrating Juneteenth
nmaahc.si.edu/blog-post/celebrating-juneteenth

Trickster Tale

Have students reflect on diverse stories and settings in this lesson about folktales.

What You Need

- ❏ *Love and Roast Chicken: A Trickster Tale from the Andes Mountains* by Barbara Knutson
- ❏ Dry-erase board and markers
- ❏ Notebook paper and pencils for students

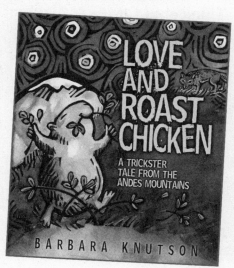

Learning Goals

- Understand what a folktale is
- Understand the significance of place in a folktale
- Brainstorm the components of a folktale rooted in students' region
- Students try writing their own folktales using agreed upon elements

Key Questions

- What is a folktale?
- Why is place and setting important in a folktale?
- What characters would be in a folktale that takes place where I live?

Talk about It

Ask students to share if they know what a folktale is. Then define the term and introduce the type of folktale you'll be working with in this lesson.

Say It

"A folktale is a story that is usually passed down by a group of people. Different countries and regions often have their own folktales that have been told for generations. One type of folktale is called a trickster tale. A trickster tale often features a small animal that outsmarts a larger animal. Let's read a trickster tale from the Andes Mountains in South America. It features a fox named Tío Antonio and a guinea pig named Cuy."

Read aloud the book *Love and Roast Chicken: A Trickster Tale from the Andes Mountains* by Barbara Knutson.

Think about It

Reaffirm the significance of place in folktales.

Say It

"Guinea pigs used to run wild in the Andes Mountains. That's why the hero of this Andes folktale is a guinea pig. If you were to write a folktale that took place where you live, what kinds of animals could be in the story?"

Try It

Come up with an idea for a new folktale together as a class.

1. Write down students' ideas for regional animal characters. Together, pick a small animal to be the trickster and a large animal to be the animal that is tricked.

2. Brainstorm and write down ideas for what the setting might be. Encourage students to think of local or regional settings, like parks or natural habitats. Have the class choose a favorite setting from the ideas.

3. Come up with desires for each of the characters. For Cuy the guinea pig, it was eating alfalfa. For Tío Antonio the fox, it was eating Cuy. Choose the ideas that students get most excited about. Don't worry about how it will logically work.

4. Tell students now that they have the basic outline of the folktale, they will each write their own version of a story featuring your chosen characters, setting, and desires.

5. After giving students a class period or two to work on their folktales, invite them to share their trickster tales with the class.

Notes

Helpful Resources

A Year Full of Stories: 52 Folk Tales and Legends from around the World by Angela McAllister

The English Schoolhouse Publishing: The Ghanaian Goldilocks
www.youtube.com/watch?v=MWhSlX66fSw&t=25s&ab_channel=TheEnglishSchoolhous
ePublishing

Shaped by Place

Explore the importance of place and setting in making us who we are.

What You Need

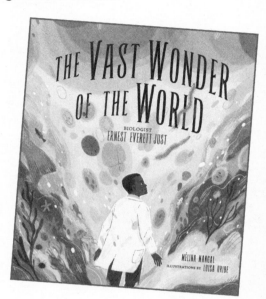

- ❑ *The Vast Wonder of the World: Biologist Ernest Everett Just* by Mélina Mangal
- ❑ Dry-erase board and markers
- ❑ Shaped by Place worksheet for each student (p. 73)

Learning Goals

- Understand some of the ways a person can be shaped by where they live
- Reflect on how the places they spend time in help make them who they are

Key Questions

- How does a place help make a person who they are?
- How am I shaped by the places I live in and visit?

Talk about It

Tell students you are going to read a book about Ernest Everett Just, a biologist who was born in South Carolina in 1883.

Say It

"Ernest lived in many places throughout his life. These places helped shape who he was and what he wanted. Let's read more about Ernest's life. As we read, listen for examples of how Ernest was influenced by where he lived."

Read aloud the book *The Vast Wonder of the World: Biologist Ernest Everett Just* by Mélina Mangal.

Think about It

Reflect on the ways in which Ernest Everett Just was shaped by where he lived. On the dry-erase board, make columns for three of the places that helped shape Just: South Carolina, New Hampshire, and Europe.

One by one, discuss with students how each place affected and shaped Just. Go back to that part of the book and have students reread important passages. Write students' ideas and observations in their respective columns. Use the example below for guidance:

South Carolina

- hurricane damaged his school; later a fire destroyed it
- segregation laws limited his rights
- rivers, marshes, and ocean sparked his interest in observing the natural world

New Hampshire

- biology class made him want to study cells

Europe

- was invited to a research institute in Germany
- felt more welcome and respected in Europe than he did in United States
- decided he could no longer put up with US segregation and moved to France

Try It

Invite students to reflect on how they are shaped by the places in their lives.

1. Give each student a copy of the Shaped by Place worksheet.
2. Ask students to think about three places they go to often. Suggest some possible ideas of places, such as home, school, grandma's house, a park, the library, a favorite diner, a place of worship, etc.
3. Have students write their three places in the spaces provided on the worksheet.
4. Below each place, ask students to share how that place shapes who they are.
5. When students are done filling out their worksheets, gather for reflection.
6. Invite students to share one of their places and what they wrote about that place.

Notes

Helpful Resources

Making Connections During Read Aloud
www.learningforjustice.org/classroom-resources/teaching-strategies/responding-to-the-readaloud-text/making-connections-during

A Sense of Place: Human Geography in the Early Childhood Classroom
www.naeyc.org/resources/pubs/yc/jul2015/sense-of-place-human-geography

Location and Place in Your Classroom
www.nationalgeographic.org/activity/location-place-your-classroom-geographic-perspective/

Shaped by Place

What places make you who you are?

Name: _____

Below, list three places you go to often. Fill in the blanks to share how each place shapes who you are.

Place 1: _____

What I do here:

Who I like here:

How I feel here:

Place 2: _____

What I do here:

Who I like here:

How I feel here:

Place 3: _____

What I do here:

Who I like here:

How I feel here:

Diversity

Classroom Kwanzaa

Learn about Kwanzaa and reflect on its seven principles with your own candle ceremony.

What You Need

- ❑ *Kevin's Kwanzaa by* Lisa Bullard
- ❑ Kwanzaa Candles printout (p. 77) and markers for coloring
- ❑ Scissors
- ❑ Tape

Learning Goals

- Learn about the Kwanzaa holiday and why it is celebrated
- Reflect on the seven principles of Kwanzaa and how they can apply to the classroom community

Key Questions

- What is Kwanzaa?
- Why and how is Kwanzaa celebrated?
- What do the seven principles of Kwanzaa mean and how might they apply to my classroom community?

Talk about It

Read aloud the book *Kevin's Kwanzaa* by Lisa Bullard.

Have students share what they remember from the book by asking the questions below. If students need prompting, go back to relevant parts of the book and reread.

What does Kwanzaa celebrate?

- Kwanzaa is a celebration of African and African American culture

Why was the holiday created?

- It was created to bring African Americans together

- It was a way to take pride in a shared African background

What are some ways people celebrate Kwanzaa?

- Putting out fruits and vegetables

- Drinking from a unity cup

- Lighting special candles

- Making presents for each other

- Gathering for food and dancing

Try It

Have students "light" the Kwanzaa candles while reflecting on the seven Kwanzaa principles.

1. Before starting the activity, copy the kinara on page 77. Cut it and the flames out separately. Color the flames, kinara, and candles.

2. Hang the Kwanzaa Candles printout on the dry-erase board. Tell students you are going to light the Kwanzaa candles together. You will light the candles in the order they are numbered.

3. Tell students that to light the candles, you need their help. Recall from the book (pp. 10–11) that each day of Kwanzaa is connected to an idea. Day one is unity. This means sticking together as a group. Ask: *Who can share an example of something our class can do together as a group?*

4. Whoever volunteers an idea, give that student one of the candle flames with tape. Let them stick the flame on the candle with the 1 above it. Write the idea they shared on the dry-erase board next to the candles.

5. Continue with the remaining six Kwanzaa principles. To add a flame to a candle, students must first answer your question. Once a student has added a flame, tell them to let others have a turn. Use the statements below to prompt students. Continue writing their answers on the dry-erase board next to the candles.

Think about It

Day 1: Unity. This means sticking together as a group. *Who can share an example of something our class can do together as a group?*

Day 2: Self-Determination. This means freedom to make our own choices. *Who can share an example of a choice we can make?*

Day 3: Collective Work and Responsibility. This means solving problems together. *Who can share an example of a problem we can solve together?*

Day 4: Cooperative Economics. This means helping and supporting one another. *Who can share an example of how we could help and support one another?*

Day 5: Purpose. This means setting goals to work toward. *Who can share an example of a goal we could work toward as a class?*

Day 6: Creativity. This means using our talents to make our community more beautiful. *Who can share an example of something beautiful we could create?*

Day 7. Faith. This means believing in ourselves and each other. *Who can share an example of how we can show faith in one another?*

Notes

2
3
4
1
5
6
7
red
red
red
black
green
green
green

Helpful Resources

The Seven Principles of Kwanzaa
nmaahc.si.edu/blog-post/seven-principles-kwanzaa

Official Kwanzaa Website
www.officialkwanzaawebsite.org/index.html

All Kinds of Rice

Explore how our heritage influences the way we cook and eat, and the importance of being open to trying new things.

What You Need
- ❑ *Everybody Cooks Rice* by Norah Dooley
- ❑ Dry-erase board and markers

Learning Goals
- Understand that families have different ways of preparing and eating meals
- Understand the importance of reacting to unfamiliar things with open curiosity

Key Questions
- What are some of the many ways that people eat rice?
- Why should I be open to things that are unfamiliar to me?
- When was a time I tried a new dish? How did I react to it?

Talk about It

Tell students you are going to read them a book called *Everybody Cooks Rice*. The book is about a neighborhood of families who come from all over the world. Every family eats rice, but they cook it in many different ways.

Ask students if their family cooks rice at home. Invite them to share how they enjoy eating rice.

Read aloud *Everybody Cooks Rice* by Norah Dooley.

Think about It

Reflect on the diversity of rice dishes portrayed in the book. *While looking for her brother at different neighbors' homes, Carrie got to taste all kinds of different rice dishes. Why were her neighbors' rice dishes different from one another?*

Ask students to remember some of the rice dishes in the book. Write their answers on the dry-erase board. Try to bring up at least four examples from the book, and make note of where the dish comes from. Use the list below to prompt students' memories.

- Rice made with black-eyed peas, fried onions, and bacon (Barbados)
- Rice made with turmeric and pigeon peas (Puerto Rico)
- Fried rice with peas and fish sauce (Vietnam)
- Rice made with peas, cashews, raisins, and spices (India)
- Steamed white rice with tofu and vegetables (China)
- Rice with red beans, chives, and hot peppers (Haiti)
- Rice with green peas and cheese (Italy)

Ask students to reflect on how Carrie reacted when offered different rice dishes.

Say It

"Carrie wasn't familiar with all of the ingredients her neighbors used. But she was open to trying the different rice dishes. Why do you think it's important to be open to things that aren't familiar to you?"

Invite students to share a time they tried a new dish. Were they unsure if they would like it? How did they react to it?

SEL Connection

It's important for young students to understand that they can be proud of their own customs while still respecting and appreciating customs they are not familiar with. Teachers can model open-minded curiosity about customs they are less familiar with by actively listening, asking questions, and verbalizing interest in the experiences of others. This modeling can apply to conversations about food customs, holiday traditions, belief systems, and more.

Helpful Resources

Modeling Curiosity and Acceptance: My Kindergarten Lunch Story
www.naeyc.org/resources/blog/modeling-curiosity-and-acceptance

Justice

Understanding Justice

Teachers know that young students have a keen sense of justice through the lens of fair and unfair. Children are also quick to pick up on differences and recognize that different people are treated differently. They may also begin to notice the way other people perceive and treat them compared to their peers.

To have a meaningful conversation about justice, it's essential to understand the injustices your students experience personally, even if they aren't yet aware of them. Injustice can be personal or systemic. Being aware of the personal and systemic injustices experienced by your students and their families will help you approach the topic with sensitivity and compassion.

Tips & Considerations

- Remind students that equal treatment does not always mean being treated the same way. For example, a person in a wheelchair might require accommodations to be treated equally to someone not in a wheelchair.

- Remind students that they should work to get to know people as individuals, rather than making assumptions.

- Bias is often unconscious—your students may not realize common thoughts or views they have are actually assumptions or stereotypes. Help them gently challenge these assumptions by asking questions about why they hold a certain view.

- When giving exemplars, avoid defaulting into stereotypes.

Questions to Ask

What are the rules in my class?

_____

_____

Are these rules fair and equitable? Why or why not?

_____

_____

Do all children have the opportunity to be successful in my class?

_____

_____

When are children allowed choice in my classroom? Do children have a say in making the class rules?

_____

_____

In what ways do I accommodate children's different ways of learning?

_____

_____

Fairness Feast

Help students build empathy and explore the concepts of fairness in a safe and constructive way as they explore the nuances of how rules can contribute to equity.

What You Need

- ❑ Dry-erase board and markers
- ❑ Fairness Feast worksheet for each group of four (pp. 85–86)
- ❑ Drawing supplies, scissors, glue sticks, and construction paper

Learning Goals

- Understand the concept of fairness
- Explore the ways rules can help make situations fair

Key Questions

- What does it mean to be fair?
- How can rules help make something fairer?
- Why are some types of rules more important than others?

Talk about It

- Begin by discussing the concept of fairness as a class. *What is fairness? What does it mean for a situation to be fair or unfair?*

Tip for Teachers

Expand on this lesson by discussing how students determined how to divide the different tasks in this activity. For example, how did they choose the spokespeople? How did they decide who would write? How did fairness contribute to these decisions?

Try It

1. Divide your class into groups of four. Explain that you will be working together to plan a Fairness Feast. Each group is responsible for creating one dish to "share" with the rest of the class.

2. Talk about what would it mean for a meal to be fair for everyone in your classroom. Offer suggestions like:
   - *There is enough food for everyone*
   - *Everyone has a food they like*
   - *There isn't any food that could make people with allergies sick*

   Invite your class to come up with additional suggestions and write them on the board.

3. Give students a few minutes to discuss what "rules" would make a meal fair for the members of their group. Remind them this could include likes and dislikes, allergies, and other requests. Have them choose the three most important rules and choose one spokesperson to share them with the class. Write each group's rules on the board. Circle any repeated rules.

4. Encourage the class to reflect on the rules list. Ask:
   - *Which rules are most important for safety reasons?*
     › Assign three points to each safety rule.
   - *Which rules were repeated in multiple groups?*
     › Assign two points to each repeated rule.
     › Assign one point to each remaining rule.

   Explain that these are fairness points.

5. Now encourage each group to plan a dish for their fairness feast, accounting for as many rules as possible. Their goal is to get the highest fairness points total while still making a dish that their own group would like to eat. They should use art supplies and construction paper to design their meal on the Fairness Feast worksheet.

6. Have each group choose a new spokesperson to share their dish with the class. They should explain why they made the choices they did. Put all the dishes on a table where students can look at them.

Think about It

Ask students to reflect on the meals and the points system:
- *What dish would you be most excited to eat?*
- *Why do you think some rules were given three fairness points and others just one?*
- *Why are some types of rules more important than others?*

Notes

Helpful Resources

One Grain of Rice: A Mathematical Folktale by Demi

What's Fair?

www.learningforjustice.org/classroom-resources/lessons/whats-fair-0

Fairness Feast

Names: _____

_____

Fairness rules: _____

_____

_____

_____

_____

_____

_____

Our meal: _____

_____

Points total: _____

Dish name: _____

Justice

Equal or Equitable?

Help students further dig into the concept of fairness by exploring the difference between equity and equality.

What You Need

- ❏ Equality vs. Equity Card for each group of three or four (p. 90)

Learning Goals

- Understand the difference between equity and equality and how it applies to fairness
- Correctly identify fair and unfair situations

Words to Know

equal: exactly the same

equitable: fair

opportunity: the chance to do or try something

Key Questions

- How is being treated fairly different from being treated the same?
- What does it mean for something to be equal?
- What does it mean for something to be equitable?

Talk about It

Tell students that today you will be exploring the idea of fairness and discussing certain situations that are fair and unfair. Explain that fairness does not always mean the same thing as being equal. Sometimes fairness means treating people differently so they can have the same opportunities. This is also known as equity.

Say It

"Equity means giving everyone equal opportunities, but it does not always mean being treated exactly the same. For example, your younger sister might need to use a stool to reach the sink to wash her hands. You don't use a stool because you can easily reach the sink without one. This is fair, even though it is not equal. In this case, you probably don't care that you don't get to use the stool, because you don't need one. But sometimes, equity can be a bit more complicated. Imagine you are riding on a city bus. The bus seats are first come first served, so the first person on can choose the first seat. You got on at an early stop, so you were able to pick your seat before the bus filled up. Now it is completely full, and you see a person using crutches get on the bus. There is nowhere for them to sit. What should you do?"

Invite the class to offer suggestions. Then encourage them to think about how offering the person your seat is an example of equity rather than equality.

Try It

1. Prior to the lesson, copy and cut out the provided equality and equity scenarios.

2. Divide students into groups of three or four. Give each group an Equality vs. Equity Card. Ask them to discuss whether their scenario is example of equity or equality. Is the situation fair or unfair? If it is unfair, how could they correct it?

3. Invite each group to select a member to read their scenario to the class. Then encourage the rest of the group to explain why they think it is an example of equity or equality. Ask the class if they agree.

Think about It

Tie the exercise back to your original discussion of fairness and equity. Ask students to reflect on what they learned about fairness and sameness after hearing the scenarios. How can treatment that isn't equal still be fair?

Notes

Helpful Resources

Equity vs Equality: What's the Difference?
www.globalcitizen.org/en/content/equity-equality-whats-the-difference-global-goals/

Fair vs. Equal
empoweringeducation.org/blog/fair-vs-equal/

Separate Is Never Equal: Sylvia Mendez and Her Family's Fight for Desegregation by Duncan Tonatiuh

Equality vs. Equity Cards

Liam's mom is deaf, so when they watch shows together, they make sure to use subtitles. The subtitles cover part of the screen, so Liam prefers to watch without them. But he knows his mom wouldn't enjoy the show as much if they turned them off.

Nora uses a wheelchair to move around. Their class is taking a field trip to a state park. It includes a hike that will be too rugged for Nora's wheelchair. So she waits in the visitor center while the rest of her class goes on the hike.

Sayid and Kia are neighbors and friends, but they go to different schools. Both schools received money to fix up their playgrounds. Sayid's school got a new playground a few years ago. It is using the money to add a few more swings and a new jungle gym. Kia's playground was very old and beginning to fall apart. Her school is going build a new playground from scratch. Kia's school received more money than Sayid's.

Isaac's parents told him and his sister, Malia, they could go to the bike park if they cleaned their rooms. Isaac did not clean his room, but Malia did. Their mom lets both kids go to the bike park.

Aurora wants to bring her dog to school, but her school has a no-pets rule. One day her class gets a new student, Zeke. He has epilepsy and has a service dog named Charley. Charley can alert Zeke if he senses a seizure coming so Zeke can get into a safe position. Charley goes everywhere with Zeke, including school. Aurora thinks it is unfair that Zeke gets to bring his dog to school and she doesn't.

Mr. Wilson gives his class a spelling test every Friday. The students get the words ahead of time and have all week to study. The students who study do well on the test and get a longer recess. One Friday, Mr. Wilson announces that all students will get a longer recess, whether or not they do well on the test.

To Be an Advocate

Students will explore what it means to be an advocate by learning about LeBron James and his advocacy work.

What You Need

- ❏ *Basketball Superstar LeBron James* by Jon M. Fishman
- ❏ Dry-erase board and markers

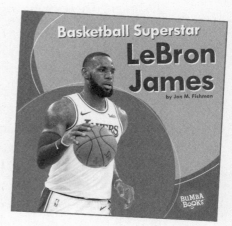

Learning Goals

- Learn about LeBron James and his activism
- Understand what it means to be an advocate
- Explore reasons why someone might choose to give back to a community

Key Questions

- What does it mean to be an advocate?
- How does James use his fame and wealth to advocate for and support different communities?
- What are some communities I am part of, and how do I support them?
- How does supporting a community help make it stronger?

Word to Know

advocate: a person who uses their status to support a cause or community

Talk about It

Tell students that today you will be learning about professional basketball player LeBron James. Engage students by inviting them to share what they know about James already. Support the discussion with details from *Basketball Superstar LeBron James* by Jon M. Fishman. Then, pivot to a discussion of James' activism and advocacy by reading aloud page 21 of the book.

Say It

"James believes education is an important part of a child's success. He saw that many students in his hometown of Akron, Ohio, were not supported in school. In 2004, he set up the LeBron James Family Foundation. This organization's goal is to help support and improve education for students in Akron. The foundation also raises money for other charities supporting kids around the country. In 2018, James helped open a school in Akron. He has also donated bikes and school supplies to Akron students and even helped pay for more than 1,000 students to attend college."

Give students the definition of an advocate. Discuss as a class some of the ways James is an advocate. After each question, list students' answers on the dry-erase board. Ask:

- *What causes and communities is James an advocate for? How does he give back to his communities? Why do you think James uses his wealth and fame to help these communities?*

Then shift the discussion to students' own communities. After each question, note students' answers on the board. Ask:

- *What communities are you part of? Do you know any advocates for these communities? How do they show their support? What are some ways you give back to your communities?*

Think about It

Encourage students to reflect on the impact of advocacy. Ask:

- *How does having members who give back strengthen a community?*

Notes

Helpful Resources

The I Promise School
ipromise.school

The LeBron James Family Foundation
www.lebronjamesfamilyfoundation.org

More Than a Vote
www.morethanavote.org

Two Voices

Students use poetry to explore empathy while learning about Japanese internment camps.

What You Need

- ❑ *A Scarf for Keiko* by Ann Malaspina
- ❑ "The Best Birthday Present: A Poem for Two Voices" by Gwendolyn Hooks, from *Thanku: Poems of Gratitude*, edited by Miranda Paul
- ❑ Speaking with Two Voices worksheet for each pair of students (p. 97)
- ❑ Paper and writing supplies for students

Learning Goals

- Introduce students to the history of Japanese internment camps
- Work with a partner to write a two-voices poem from the perspective of each character in a book

Key Questions

- How does looking at an event from two perspectives change my view of it?
- What can we learn from studying history from two perspectives?
- What role should empathy play when learning about historical events?

Talk about It

Explain that today you will be talking about Japanese internment camps. Provide context for the rest of your discussion.

Consider This

Some students may have anxiety about reading work aloud to the class. Be respectful of students' choice to not share their poems.

Say It

"From 1939 to 1945, much of the world was involved in World War II. On December 7, 1941, Japanese forces bombed US military base Pearl Harbor. Soon after, the US government decided that Japanese Americans could not be trusted. It ordered all Japanese Americans into internment camps."

Read *A Scarf for Keiko* by Ann Malaspina aloud to your class. Discuss the book as a class with the following questions, or ask your own:

* *Why did Sam's brother not want him to talk to Keiko? Was this fair or unfair?*
* *Why do you think Keiko knit Sam a scarf? How do you think this made Sam feel?*
* *Why do you think Sam knit Keiko a scarf? How do you think this made Keiko feel?*
* *Why was it unfair that Keiko and her family were forced to go to the internment camp?*

Try It

1. Divide your students into pairs and give each pair the Speaking with Two Voices worksheet. Say that they will be working together with their partners to write a two-voices poem. Explain that a two-voices poem is a poem meant for two people to read out loud. The lines of the poem are divided into two columns. Each column represents a different speaker. Sometimes a poet wants both speakers to say the same thing at the same time. Then the word or phrase appears in both columns. These poems often read like a script or a conversation between two people.

2. Invite two students to read aloud "The Best Birthday Present: A Poem for Two Voices" by Gwendolyn Hooks, from *Thanku: Poems of Gratitude*, edited by Miranda Paul. Show students the page, so they can see how the poem appears visually.

3. Explain that each pair of students is going to write a two-voices poem. One voice will be Keiko's, and the other will be Sam's. As students work, visit each pair to answer questions and offer advice or suggestions as needed.

4. Invite each pair or call on pairs to read their poems aloud to the class.

Think about It

Reflect on what students learned after writing their poems and listening to their classmates' poetry. Do they feel any differently about their answers from the original discussion questions you asked? How did writing from Keiko's or Sam's point of view affect their answers?

SEL Connection

Acknowledging the importance of other viewpoints and perspectives is a key component to building empathy. Throughout this activity, encourage students to actively consider Keiko's and Sam's perspectives. Rather than just considering how students might feel if they were in Keiko's or Sam's situation, encourage students to look for clues in the book that hint at how the characters are thinking.

Notes

Speaking with Two Voices

Names: _____

Poem title: _____

Keiko	Sam
_____	_____
_____	_____
_____	_____
_____	_____
_____	_____
_____	_____
_____	_____
_____	_____
_____	_____

Buddy Interview

Help students learn to unpack assumptions and get to know one another as individuals.

What You Need

- ❏ About My Buddy worksheet for each student (p. 101)
- ❏ Writing supplies for students

Learning Goals

- Understand the definition of prejudice and assumptions and why both are problematic
- Ask respectful questions to get to know a classmate as an individual

Key Questions

- What is an assumption?
- How can I get to know someone as an individual rather than making an assumption about them?

Talk about It

Explain that today you will be talking about prejudice and about why it is important to get to know people as individuals rather than making assumptions about them. Give an example from your own life, such as, *Because I'm Hispanic, some people assume I love tamales, but really, my favorite food is pizza!*

Words to Know

assumption: something that is believed without proof

prejudice: a pre-existing opinion not based on facts or experience

Consider This

Do you make assumptions about your students based on how they look, their gender, or their socioeconomic status? How can you challenge these assumptions and learn about your students as individuals?

Say It

"Prejudice means to 'pre-judge' someone. This means you make assumptions about another person without getting to know them. These assumptions might be based on how someone looks, a group they are part of, or even your own experience. These assumptions may be positive or negative. But they are always unfair. We can't know what someone else likes or dislikes or what they are thinking or feeling unless we get to know them as an individual. The best way to get to know people is by asking respectful questions. Our class is full of unique individuals. That's what makes it fun and exciting! Today, we're going to practice asking each other respectful questions to learn more about one another as individuals."

Try It

1. Give each student the About My Buddy worksheet.

2. Divide students into random pairs. Give students time to fill out the first to columns of the worksheet. Remind them to make sure the items in the "What I Know" column are not assumptions.

3. Have one student in each pair interview their buddy using the questions in the second column. Have them fill out the third column with their answers.

4. Have the interviewer and interviewee switch roles.

Think about It

Come back together as a class. Invite students to share what they learned during their conversation.

- *What do you and your buddy have in common?*

- *What makes your buddy unique?*

- *What surprised you most about your buddy?*

- *How did it feel to have someone else learn about you as an individual?*

Notes

About My Buddy

My name: _____

My buddy's name: _____

What I Know	What I Want to Know	What I Learned

Understanding Action

In the minds of young learners, an activist or leader likely takes the shape of an adult who stands at podiums, speaks to crowds, or gives orders. Students may not understand the small ways in which they, as young people, can exemplify leadership and activism. By providing students today with some building blocks of action—including empathy, allyship, and a sense of justice—we set them up to be tomorrow's leaders.

To encourage students to take action as leaders, reflect on how you model leadership as a teacher. Do you listen to students, acknowledge their ideas, and support their efforts? Do you believe in all students and hold them to the same expectations? How can you build the confidence of students who don't see themselves as leaders?

Tips & Considerations

- Before students can consider themselves leaders, they need to feel assured of their value and abilities. Recognize and reinforce each student's strengths. When possible, verbalize what that student excels at or has to offer.

- When discussing leaders and activists, use examples of individuals across different cultures and identity groups.

- Give students small opportunities to be leaders in the classroom: have them pass out materials, lead everyone to lunch, keep time during an activity, etc.

- A teacher's unconscious bias can influence how much they expect from and demand of their students. Students pick up on cues that adults expect more from them, and their self-worth and learning potential benefits.

Questions to Ask

What are my students' strengths?

_____

_____

_____

Who is a natural leader in the class? What are the qualities of this student?

_____

_____

_____

Who is shy in the class? How might I help this child step into their own leadership abilities?

_____

_____

_____

What are my expectations for all students?

_____

_____

_____

Working as a Team

Learn about solving problems as a group using the inspiring example of Prasit Hemmin and his floating soccer field.

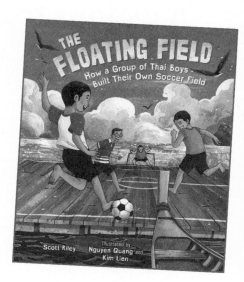

What You Need

- ❑ *The Floating Field: How a Group of Thai Boys Built Their Own Soccer Field* by Scott Riley
- ❑ Prasit's Floating Field worksheet for each student (p. 106)
- ❑ Writing supplies for students

Learning Goals

- Learn about how Prasit Hemmin and his friends solved a problem together
- Reflect on times students solved a problem with a group

Key Questions

- What is a problem I solved with a group, and how did we solve it?
- What is problem I would like to solve? How could I work with a group to solve it?

Talk about It

Tell students you are going to read a book about Prasit Hemmin's soccer team in Thailand.

Say It

"Prasit and his friends lived in Koh Panyee, a village on a tiny island off the coast of Thailand. There was no room in the small village for a soccer field. So Prasit and his friends decided to build a field that could float on the water! Let's read their story."

Read aloud the book *The Floating Field: How a Group of Thai Boys Built Their Own Soccer Field* by Scott Riley.

Think about It

When you are finished reading, give each student a copy of the Prasit's Floating Field worksheet. Give them time to write their answers to each question.

When students have completed their worksheets, go through the questions together and discuss their answers.

Q: Why could Prasit and his friends only play soccer when the tide was low?
A: The low tide exposed the sandbar they played on.

Q: What is the solution Prasit and his friends came up with so they could play soccer more?
A: They decided to build a field that could float on the water.

Q: What was one outcome of Prasit and his friends building the field together?
A: 1) They were able to play whenever they wanted; 2) They were able to train for competitive play; 3) They formed the Panyee Football Club; 4) They got third place in their first tournament.

Invite students to share their responses to the last two questions on the worksheet.

Notes

Prasit's Floating Field *

Answer the questions below about the book *The Floating Field*.

Name: _____

Why could Prasit and his friends only play soccer when the tide was low? _____

What is the solution Prasit and his friends came up with so they could play soccer more? _____
_____

What was one outcome of Prasit and his friends building the field together? _____
_____

Think of a time you worked with others to solve a problem. What was the problem, and what was your solution? _____
_____
_____

What is a problem you would like to solve? How might you solve it with a group? _____
_____

Active Listening

Help students understand and practice active listening with a partner activity.

What You Need

- ☐ Dry-erase board and markers

Learning Goals

- Understand what it means to listen to others
- Understand what it looks like to listen to others
- Practice actively listening to a partner

Key Questions

- What is the difference between hearing and listening?
- How do I show someone I am listening to them?
- How does it feel to be listened to?

Talk about It

Introduce to students the importance of listening to others.

Say It

"When we work and play with others, we need to know how to listen to them. When we listen to someone, we are doing more than just hearing them. We are giving them our full attention and thinking about what they are saying to us."

Ask students to think about ways they show someone they are listening. Write their ideas on the dry-erase board. Use the following list as a guide:

- body turned toward theirs
- make eye contact
- lean toward them
- nod head
- make sounds or statements of affirmation, such as "I see"
- ask follow-up questions

Point out to students that we cannot simply give the appearance of listening to someone. We have to pay attention to and think about what they are saying.

Try It

Have students practice active listening through repetition and follow-up questioning.

1. Divide the students into pairs. Have one student tell about their day so far, from the time they woke up until now. After each statement the speaker makes, the listener should repeat it back in the second person. For example, if the speaker says, "I almost missed the bus because I couldn't find my math book," the listener will say, "You almost missed the bus because you couldn't find your math book."

2. After a few minutes, tell students to switch roles in their pairs. Repeat step 1 in their new roles.

3. After a few minutes, tell students to switch roles again. This time, the speaker will talk about what they plan to do for the rest of the day, from now until they go to bed. Instead of repeating back each statement, the listener will ask the speaker at least two follow-up questions about things they shared.

4. After a few minutes, go around the room and have each listener share one thing the speaker told them.

5. Have students switch roles one last time before repeating steps 3 and 4.

Think about It

Reflect as a group on how the exercise went. Ask students to share how they could tell their partner was listening to them. Ask them how it felt to know they were being listened to.

Notes

Helpful Resources

To Sustain the Tough Conversations, Active Listening Must Be the Norm
www.learningforjustice.org/magazine/to-sustain-the-tough-conversations-active
-listening-must-be-the-norm

Tips & Activities to Improve Your Child's Active Listening Skills
www.oxfordlearning.com/improve-active-listening-skills/

Showing Kindness

Help students use empathy to show kindness to others.

Learning Goals

- Understand what empathy means
- Practice showing empathy

Key Questions

- What is empathy?
- What does empathy look like?

Tip for Teachers

Consider doing this lesson after Active Listening (pp. 107-109) so you can build on it, teaching students that we can go a step beyond active listening by showing empathy.

Talk about It

If you've already completed the Active Listening lesson (pp. 107-109) and it is fresh in students' brains, use it as a jumping-off point for this activity.

Say It

"Remember when we practiced listening to each other and showing with our faces and bodies that we were listening? One reason it's important to listen is so we can practice empathy. Empathy is the feeling of understanding what someone else is experiencing or feeling.

"Imagine your friend got a bad grade on a test. She's feeling upset. How might you show her kindness?"

Brainstorm ways to show kindness in the above scenario. Point out to students that everyone prefers to be shown kindness in different ways. It's important to listen to what our friend needs most in the moment.

- give her space
- invite her to play at recess
- give her a hug
- try to make her laugh
- offer to help her study
- share your snack

Think about It

Share the following scenarios with students. After each, reflect on the feelings of the characters involved.

Mario sits at a table with his friends at lunch. He sees his new classmate, Theresa, sitting by herself at the next table.
How might Theresa be feeling? How can Mario show kindness?

Jamal and his little sister Salma go to the fair. Salma wins a stuffed turtle as a prize at one of the fair games. Jamal does not win a prize.
How might Jamal be feeling? How can Salma show kindness? How might Salma be feeling? How can Jamal show kindness?

Hope wants to play catch with her dad after school. But Hope's dad has had to work late a lot. He is usually too tired to play when he comes home.
How might Hope's dad be feeling? How can Hope show her dad kindness?

Notes

Helpful Resources

Personal Health Series: Empathy
classroom.kidshealth.org/classroom/3to5/personal/growing/empathy.pdf

Understanding Empathy
www.learningforjustice.org/classroom-resources/lessons/understanding-empathy

Expressing Gratitude

Learn about expressing gratitude through different forms of poetry.

What You Need

- ❑ *Thanku: Poems of Gratitude* edited by Miranda Paul
- ❑ Paper and writing supplies for students

Learning Goals

- Understand that showing gratitude is a bold action
- Learn about a few of the different forms a gratitude poem can take
- Practice writing a poem of gratitude

Key Questions

- What am I grateful for?
- What is a way I can express my gratitude?

Talk about It

Introduce to students the idea that expressing gratitude is an important form of taking action. *Sometimes, especially when we're having a bad day, the boldest action we can take is showing gratitude for all the good things we have.*

Present to students *Thanku: Poems of Gratitude* edited by Miranda Paul.

Say It

"This is a collection of different types of poems by different authors. We're going to read a few of the poems from this collection. As I read, make note of the poems you especially like. Write down words or phrases that stood out to you."

Read a selection of poems from *Thanku: Poems of Gratitude*. Consider including the following in your reading:

- "Thank You, Sleep!" by Carolyn Dee Flores
- "Atta-Dude" by Sarvinder Naberhaus
- "Alice Thanks the Looking Glass(es)" by Patti Richards
- "Dimples" by Chrystal D. Giles
- "The Perfect Rock" by Jamie McGillen
- "All This" by Liz Garton Scanlon

Think about It

When you are done reading the selection, ask students to share which poems they liked best. Invite them to share any words or phrases they wrote down while listening.

Try It

Have students write their own acrostic poems.

1. Revisit the poem "Dimples" by Chrystal D. Giles. Tell students this is an example of an acrostic poem. The first letters of the lines combine to spell out the word dimples, which is what the poet is expressing gratitude for.

2. Tell students to think of something they are grateful for. Have them write that word in capital letters vertically down the left side of their paper.

3. Tell students to write the first line of the poem from the top letter. The line can be a phrase or a single word describing the thing they are thankful for.

4. Have students repeat step 3 for each letter of their vertical word.

5. When students are finished writing, invite them to share their acrostic poems with the group.

Notes

Helpful Resources

11 Classroom Activities to Teach Students Gratitude
www.imaginelearning.com/blog/2018/11/11-classroom-activities-teach-students
-gratitude

Sharing Our Colors: Writing Poetry
www.learningforjustice.org/classroom-resources/lessons/sharing-our-colors-writing
-poetry

Act of Compassion

Encourage students to show compassion for those who are struggling.

What You Need

- ❏ *A Map into the World* by Kao Kalia Yang
- ❏ Drawing paper and supplies for students

Learning Goals

- Understand the meaning of compassion
- Practice showing compassion for someone who needs it

Key Questions

- What is compassion?
- How can I act with compassion when I see someone who is struggling?

Talk about It

Tell students you are going to read a book about showing compassion. *Compassion is caring and showing concern for others who are suffering. Feeling compassion makes us want to do something to ease the suffering of others.*

Read aloud the book *A Map into the World* by Kao Kalia Yang.

Tip for Teachers

The copyright page of *A Map into the World* includes a small Hmong pronunciation guide.

Think about It

Reflect on the main character's act of compassion. Ask students to answer the following questions:

- *Who did the main character of the book, Paj Ntaub, show compassion for?*
- *Why did Paj Ntaub feel compassion for her neighbor Bob?*
- *What action did Paj Ntaub take to ease the suffering of her neighbor Bob?*

Try It

Have students practice compassion with this activity inspired by *A Map into the World*.

1. Give each student a sheet of drawing paper and drawing supplies.

2. Recall how Paj Ntaub drew pictures of the things she saw around her home, such as plants, leaves, her brothers, an airplane, and snowflakes. She called this a "map into the world."

3. Tell students to create maps into their worlds. Draw items that they often see that have become part of their worlds.

4. Instruct students to save the maps they create. Next time they encounter someone who is struggling or suffering, give this person their map as an act of compassion.

Notes

Helpful Resources

The Compassion Project
thecompassionproject.com/

What Is Compassion?
www.learningforjustice.org/classroom-resources/lessons/what-is-compassion

Acceptance and Friendship

Discuss with students what it means to accept our friends for who they are.

What You Need

- ❑ *Yaffa and Fatima: Shalom, Salaam* by Fawzia Gilani-Williams
- ❑ Dry-erase board and markers
- ❑ My Friend worksheet for each student (p. 120)
- ❑ Writing supplies for students

Learning Goals

- Understand what it looks like to accept someone who is different from us
- Think of ways we show acceptance to our own friends

Key Questions

- What does it mean to accept someone?
- What does it look like to show acceptance and friendship?
- How do I show acceptance to my friend?

Talk about It

Tell students you are going to read a story about friendship and acceptance. *Accepting someone means appreciating them as they are and not asking them to change.*

Read aloud *Yaffa and Fatima: Shalom, Salaam* by Fawzia Gilani-Williams.

Think about It

Ask students to name some of the ways Yaffa and Fatima were different. List their thoughts on the dry-erase board.

- They made different types of food (shawarma and schnitzel)
- They prayed in different places (synagogue and mosque)
- They read different holy books (Siddur and Qur'an)

- They observed different holidays (Yom Kippur/Passover and Ramadan/Eid)
- They had different ways of saying "Peace!" (Shalom/Salaam)

Ask students to share some examples of Yaffa and Fatima showing friendship and accepting each other. List their thoughts on the dry-erase board.

- They had meals together
- They greeted one another by waving and saying "Peace" in different languages
- They showed concern that the other had enough to eat
- They gave each other the food they had, even when neither had much to give
- They showed love and gratitude for the other's generosity

Try It

Ask students to reflect on how they show acceptance in their own friendships.

1. Give each student a copy of the My Friend worksheet.

2. Have students think about a good friend of theirs. Ask them to share a bit about their friendship by filling in the worksheet.

3. When students have completed their worksheets, invite them to share with the class what they shared on the worksheet.

Notes

Helpful Resources

One Nation, Many Beliefs
www.learningforjustice.org/classroom-resources/lessons/one-nation-many-beliefs

Celebrating Differences: Five Lessons for Teaching Kids Acceptance
www.poehealth.org/celebrating-differences/

My Friend

Think about a good friend of yours. Share a bit about your friendship below!

My name: _____

My friend's name: _____

Some ways my friend and I are different:

_____

_____

_____

Some things I appreciate about my friend:

_____

_____

_____

How I show my friend that I appreciate them:

_____

_____

_____

Being a Leader

Explore with students what it means to be a good leader.

What You Need

- ❏ Dry-erase board and markers
- ❏ *Michelle Obama: Political Icon* by Heather E. Schwartz

Learning Goals

- Think about what makes a good leader
- Think about some ways to lead at home, at school, or in the community

Key Questions

- What does it take to be a good leader?
- What are some small ways in which I can show leadership?

Talk about It

Ask students to share what they think makes a good leader. Write their ideas on the dry-erase board. If they need help, prompt them with some examples:

- Listens to the ideas of others
- Includes everyone
- Treats others fairly
- Is friendly and encouraging
- Takes initiative/acts on ideas
- Shows/teaches others how to do something

Read aloud *Michelle Obama: Political Icon* by Heather E. Schwartz.

Think about It

Reflect on Michelle Obama's journey to becoming a leader. Obama became a national political leader when she became First Lady of the United States in 2008. But she showed she could be a leader long before that. What are some ways in which Obama showed leadership early in life? Write students' answers on the dry-erase board. They may include any or all of the following:

- She decided she wanted to learn piano and took charge of learning advanced songs on her own
- She made sure to correct her mistakes in school
- She took part in extra school activities, like attending a community college writing class and dissecting a rat
- She was a member of student council in high school
- She worked to get accepted at Princeton University even when her school counselor discouraged her
- She founded a program that prepared young people for jobs in public service
- She created a community service program at the University of Chicago

Ask students to write down some small ways they can show leadership at home, at school, or in their greater community, such as their neighborhood.

When students have finished writing, invite them to share some of their ideas.

Notes

Community Action

Inspire students to take action in their communities by reading Isatou Ceesay's story.

What You Need

- ❏ *One Plastic Bag: Isatou Ceesay and the Recycling Women of the Gambia* by Miranda Paul
- ❏ Dry-erase board and markers
- ❏ Taking Action worksheet for each student (p. 125)
- ❏ Writing supplies for students

Learning Goals

- Learn a true story of taking action to make a community cleaner and healthier
- Think about the process of recognizing a problem and coming up with a solution
- Engage in problem solving using one's own community as an example

Key Questions

- What is an example of community action?
- What is a problem in my community?
- What is one possible solution to the problem, and how can I personally help?

Talk about It

Tell students you are going to read a story about a young woman who took action to make a difference in her community.

Read aloud *One Plastic Bag: Isatou Ceesay and the Recycling Women of the Gambia* by Miranda Paul.

Think about It

Reflect on what you just read by asking students the following questions. Write their answers on the dry-erase board.

- *What problem did Isatou Ceesay notice in her community?*
- *Why was it a problem?*
- *What idea did Isatou come up with the solve the problem?*
- *What is one change that took place as a result of Isatou's action?*

Try It

Ask students to contemplate an action they can take in their communities.

1. Give each student a copy of the Taking Action worksheet.

2. Have students reflect on an action they could take in their own communities by answering the questions on the worksheet.

3. Once everyone has completed the worksheet, gather for reflection.

4. Invite students to share the ideas they came up with.

Notes

Taking Action

Isatou Ceesay noticed a problem in her community and took action.

Name: _____

1. What is a problem you have noticed in your community?

_____

_____

2. Why is it a problem? _____

_____

_____

_____

3. What is one way this problem could be solved? _____

_____

_____

4. What is something you can personally do to help fix the problem?

_____

_____

_____

Notes

Notes

Acknowledgments

The images in this book are used with the permission of: © andreswd/iStockphoto, p. 45; © AnnaStills/iStockphoto, p. 26; © Arcady/Shutterstock Images, pp. 5 (fingerprint icon), 19 (fingerprint icon); © bsd/Shutterstock Images, pp. 5 (hand icons), 20 (hand icons); © Devita ayu silvianingtyas/Shutterstock Images, p. 77; © FatCamera/iStockphoto, pp. 6, 20 (teacher and boy), 34 (girl reading), 99, 121 (group of kids); © ferrantraite/iStockphoto, p. 12 (portrait of a little girl praying); © FG Trade/iStockphoto, p. 10; © GagliardiPhotography/Shutterstock Images, p. 65 (girl raising hand); © irysha/ Shutterstock Images, pp. 5 (star doodles), 22 (star doodles); © kali9/iStockphoto, pp. 4, 21 (students on bus); © kate_sept2004/iStockphoto, p. 14; © katleho Seisa/iStockphoto, p. 13; © Lerner Publishing Group, Inc., pp. 12 (*Dictionary for a Better World* book cover), 19 (*Yaffa and Fatima* book cover), 20 (*Niko Draws a Feeling* book cover), 21 (*Book Itch* book cover), 22 (*One Plastic Bag* book cover), 25, 34 (*Who Is a Scientist* book cover), 43 (*Misty Copeland* book cover), 46, 50, 53, 61, 64, 67, 70, 74, 78, 91 (*LeBron James* book cover), 94, 104, 112, 115, 117, 121 (*Michelle Obama* book cover), 123 (*One Plastic Bag* book cover); © LightField Studios/Shutterstock Images, p. 16; © LumiNola/iStockphoto, pp. 87, 113; © Memedozaslan/iStockphoto, p. 22 (students developing a robot); © Michele Pevide/iStockphoto, p. 91 (reading a book); © MIND AND I/Shutterstock Images, p. 75; © monkeybusinessimages/iStockphoto, pp. 29, 58; © Moyo Studio/iStockphoto, p. 38; © Ridofranz/iStockphoto, p. 65 (children reading from a notebook); © SDI Productions/ iStockphoto, pp. 47, 107; © Six_Characters/iStockphoto, p. 82; © VioletaStoimenova/ iStockphoto, p. 123 (girl using laptop); © Visual Generation/Shutterstock Images, pp. 5 (justice icon), 21 (justice icon), 86; © Wavebreakmedia/iStockphoto, pp. 18, 43 (children reading books), 80, 118.

Cover Photos: © FatCamera/iStockphoto, (teacher and group of kids); © Wavebreakmedia/ iStockphoto (student in wheelchair)

Design Elements: © Meowlina Meow/Shutterstock Images (doodles); © Mighty Media, Inc. (curvy lines); © Nazarkru/Shutterstock Images (abstract background)